THE ROYAL HORTICULTURAL SOCIETY
PRACTICAL GUIDES

CLEMATIS

THE ROYAL HORTICULTURAL SOCIETY
PRACTICAL GUIDES

CLEMATIS

CHARLES CHESSHIRE

DORLING KINDERSLEY

LONDON • NEW YORK • SYDNEY • MOSCOW
www.dk.com

A DORLING KINDERSLEY BOOK
www.dk.com

PROJECT EDITOR Samantha Gray
ART EDITOR Rachael Parfitt

SERIES EDITOR Pamela Brown
SERIES ART EDITOR Stephen Josland

MANAGING EDITOR Louise Abbott
MANAGING ART EDITOR Lee Griffiths

DTP DESIGNER Matthew Greenfield

PRODUCTION MANAGER Patricia Harrington

First published in Great Britain in 1999
by Dorling Kindersley Limited,
9 Henrietta Street, London WC2E 8PS

Copyright © 1999 Dorling Kindersley Limited, London

A CIP catalogue for this book is available from the British Library.
ISBN 0 7513 0686X

Reproduced by Colourpath, London
Printed and bound by Star Standard Industries, Singapore

CONTENTS

USING CLEMATIS IN THE GARDEN

WHICH CLEMATIS WHERE?

CLEMATIS ARE SO VERSATILE that even in the smallest garden there are many more possibilities for growing them than most of us realize. With the huge range of species and more than 400 cultivars to choose from, deciding which to grow is both exciting and a bit bewildering. Pick the right one and it will climb to the tree tops or live happily in a pot. It is this versatility, combined with the great variety in flower shape and colour, that makes clematis so popular.

TYPES OF FLOWER

Flower shapes range from the gentle, nodding blooms of many of the species clematis to the big, bold showstoppers found among the large-flowered hybrids. As a very rough guide, clematis can be divided into these two major groupings.

With blooms that measure anything up to 20cm in diameter, it is the large-flowered hybrids that have been bred to put on a dazzling display through summer.

The flowers are usually single but there are also several doubles. The clematis that are usually referred to as species clematis tend to have smaller flowers of more varied shape that appear in the spring, late summer and autumn. They include, among others, *Clematis armandii, C. alpina, C. macropetala, C. montana, C. texensis, C. viticella, C. tibetana* and *C. tangutica*. A photographic gallery (*see p.49*) illustrates the range and gives their flowering times.

THE VARIETY OF FLOWER SHAPES

In size, the large-flowered hybrids are followed by C. montana *and* C. viticella. *Of the smaller species* C. armandii *has typically saucer-shaped flowers,* C. alpina *open bells,* C. tangutica *closed bells, and* C. texensis *tulip-shaped flowers.*

LARGE-FLOWERED HYBRID (SINGLE)

LARGE-FLOWERED HYBRID (DOUBLE)

CLEMATIS MONTANA

CLEMATIS VITICELLA

SAUCER-SHAPED

OPEN BELL-SHAPED

BELL-SHAPED

TULIP-SHAPED

◀ PINK PARTNERS *The large-flowered hybrid 'Comtesse de Bouchaud' with the rose 'Pink Bells'.*

FAMILY ORIGINS

Initially, plant breeders concentrated on the large-flowered hybrids. George Jackman, a nurseryman, produced 'Jackmanii', one of the first and still one of the most popular, in 1862. Since then, hybridizers around the world have been busy extending the range and in recent years have turned their attention to the species, introducing many splendid new plants.

Clematis belong to the same plant family as buttercups, peonies and anemones. There are over 200 species distributed around the world but the majority hail from the temperate regions of the northern hemisphere. The eye-catching flowers are not actually composed of petals but sepals. Most flowers have two layers surrounding the stamens – the green sepals that protect the flowerbud and coloured petals that attract insects. In a few plants, however, such as clematis, it is the sepals that are coloured, looking just like petals.

HOW THEY GROW

The majority of clematis are climbers and, for the most part, that is how we prize them, growing them up trellises and

▲ OVER THE GATE
'Perle d'Azur' makes a welcoming arch. It is one of the finest of the large-flowered hybrids that bloom in the second half of summer.

◀ SWAGS OF RED
'Kermesina' puts on a magnificent show from late summer to autumn. This is a good clematis to grow among shrubs.

pergolas, or around arches and gateways. But it is, above all, their natural ability to grow through and with other plants that makes clematis invaluable. In the wild, they use other plants for support, scrambling through trees and shrubs by twisting their leaf stalks around the twigs. They are often at their best seen growing in this way, and it is an ideal method to adopt in the garden. Clematis can also be used to hide ugly buildings or as ground cover. They can be planted in pots on a patio and, in addition, there are several truly herbaceous clematis, excellent for borders and beds.

THROUGH THE SEASONS

By selecting from the many species and hybrids it is possible to have a long succession of different clematis flowers. Some produce beautiful fluffy seedheads, like those on C. *vitalba*, the "old man's beard" of British hedgerows. Those that follow the autumn flowers of C. *tibetana*, C. *tangutica* and 'Bill MacKenzie' extend the season even further. The clematis palette includes every colour except bright orange. Fragrance is elusive in all but a few of the species and many of those are the more tender varieties. Clematis are generally hardy, especially most of the large-flowered

Clematis are in the same family as field buttercups and garden peonies

hybrids and C. *alpina*, which can withstand down to -30°C. Many grow well in shade or on north walls and they thrive in most soils, although they prefer moisture-retentive conditions and good nutrition.

BORDER TIME
The clouds of tiny white flowers of Clematis recta, *a herbaceous species, add substance to a planting that includes the purple spikes of a salvia, an old-fashioned pink rose and fennel.*

THE CLEMATIS YEAR

A CAREFUL SELECTION of about a dozen species and hybrids will almost guarantee that you have at least one clematis in flower in the garden from early spring to autumn. Many types also have the advantage of feathery seedheads to follow the flowers, and some have fern-like or young purple foliage (*see chart, facing page*). To help you choose a mixture of clematis that will provide a succession of flowers, the gallery at the back of this book has been arranged in order of flowering season.

STARTING THE SEASON

For colour at the start of the year, there are species that flower in late winter and early spring in mild areas or in a conservatory. Provide evergreen *Clematis cirrhosa* with some protection and you will be rewarded by freckled, cream bells in late winter. By early spring, evergreen *C. armandii* and *C. indivisa* give a display of fragrant white

> ### Shining, fluffy seedheads in autumn extend the clematis season

flowers. Both need the shelter of a wall. The hardy alpinas and macropetalas also flower in early spring, producing seedheads to follow. Flowers vary from the simple bells of *C. alpina* to the intricate, nodding flowers of *C. macropetala*. By late spring,

▲ SWEET BEGINNINGS
Clematis armandii *carries clusters of flowers in early spring, which stand out well against the leathery evergreen leaves. A warm, sunny day will bring out their almond scent.*

◄ SPRING CHARM
Clematis alpina *'Rosy Pagoda' is an attractive and delicate-looking cultivar of this extremely hardy early-flowering species.*

SUMMERTIME BLUES
'Lady Londesborough', an early large-flowered hybrid, is closely related to the species Clematis patens, *used to breed many in this group.*

AUTUMN HIGHLIGHTS
The seedheads of Clematis tibetana *are among the most lustrous of any clematis, especially when caught by rays of autumn sunshine.*

the vigorous *C. montana* is in flower and some large-flowered hybrids, such as 'Lady Londesborough' (*above*), produce their first flush. Many flower again in late summer and early autumn, but their main flowering time is from late spring into early summer.

FROM SUMMER INTO AUTUMN

In summer, the large-flowered hybrids give a long display of blooms. Two groups dominate late summer – the large-flowered Jackmanii types and small-flowered viticellas. *C. viticella* starts to bloom earlier than the red-flowered *C. texensis*, while hybrids of the two offer an extended flowering season and a range of flower shapes and colours.

Many herbaceous and species clematis also flower in late summer. Two of the most popular climbing species are *C. tangutica* and *C. tibetana* subsp. *vernayi* (previously known as *C. orientalis*), which produce small, yellow bells, followed by seedheads. The herbaceous *C. heracleifolia* and its varieties also flower in late summer. These are often fragrant and have the advantage of handsome, ground-covering foliage.

CLEMATIS WITH EXTRA SEASONAL INTEREST

HANDSOME FOLIAGE

These all have leaves that are particularly attractive even when the plant is not in flower:

C. aethusifolia Fern-like leaves
C. akebioides Fern-like leaves
C. cirrhosa var. *balearica* Finely cut evergreen foliage, turning bronze in winter
C. intricata Fern-like leaves
C. tibetana Blue-green, finely cut foliage
C. recta 'Purpurea' Purple foliage, turning green later in the season

DECORATIVE SEEDHEADS

The following all develop fluffy seedheads that enhance the plant long after flowering:

Alpinas (*see pages 50–51*)
Macropetalas (*see pages 50–51*)
C. ladakhiana
C. tibetana (*see photograph above*)
C. tangutica
C. vitalba
'Bill MacKenzie'

THE COLOUR RANGE

WITH ALMOST THE ENTIRE spectrum to choose from, clematis offer the gardener a vast selection of colours, from pale, subtle or dark shades to vivid, intense ones. Flowers vary from the small, primrose-scented, creamy-green bells of *Clematis rehderiana* to the velvety, deep crimson blooms of the large-flowered hybrid 'Niobe' (*below*).

CLEMATIS TANGUTICA

COLOUR THROUGH THE SEASONS

There is a white-flowered clematis for nearly every time of the year, from *Clematis armandii* in early spring, *C. alpina* 'White Moth', *C. montana* f. *grandiflora*, 'Miss Bateman', 'Alba Luxurians' and 'Huldine' through spring and summer, to 'Paul Farges' in autumn. 'Marie Boisselot' has white flowers with cream stamens, while 'Miss Bateman' and 'James Mason' have purple stamens. Many of the wild species, such as the fragrant *C. flammula* and *C. potaninii*, have small white flowers. The coloured foliage of the herbaceous *C. recta* 'Purpurea' is an ideal foil for its tiny white flowers in summer, while the white alpinas have pale green leaves.

The flower colours of pale pink, pale mauve and silvery-blue hybrids, such as 'Silver Moon', 'Dawn', 'Miss Crawshay'

THE CLEMATIS PALETTE
As a genus, clematis provide the gardener with an extraordinary range of colours to choose from. Flowers vary from the purest white to the deepest, richest purple and often have prominent, colourful stamens that complement or contrast with the petals. A few clematis have dark foliage that sets off the flowers to even greater advantage.

CLEMATIS REHDERIANA

'MARIE BOISSELOT'

'NIOBE'

'ROYALTY'

'THE VAGABOND'

and 'Wada's Primrose', are likely to fade in bright sunlight, so it is best to plant them in light shade or next to a north wall. Pale early-flowering species, such as *C. montana* and *C. alpina*, flower when the sun is not so strong and are therefore less prone to fading. The purple-pink flowers of

Red flowers are at their best in full sun, pale colours need shade

C. montana 'Tetrarose' and 'Warwickshire Rose' have the advantage of bronze young foliage to set them off.

The dark hybrids, particularly the purples of the Jackmanii group and the near-true blues, such as 'Mrs Cholmondeley' and 'Perle d'Azur', tend to flower most profusely in full sun, although 'Fireworks' and 'Lady Northcliffe' retain their flower colour best when there is a little overhead shade.

The red-flowered hybrids, including 'Ville de Lyon', 'Rouge Cardinal', 'Niobe' and 'Ernest Markham', and the viticella types, such as 'Kermesina' and 'Madame Julia Correvon', flower most profusely and gain their best colour intensity in full sun.

While there are cream large-flowered hybrids, the only true yellow clematis are in the tibetana group, producing small bells from mid- to late summer. The best choices are *C. tibetana*, *C. tangutica* and 'Bill MacKenzie', which have fluffy seedheads after flowering. They are usually vigorous and suitable for growing up small trees or through shrubs. Softer yellow *C. serratifolia* is another late-flowering clematis.

CLEMATIS ALPINA 'WILLY'

'JOHN WARREN'

'COMTESSE DE BOUCHAUD'

'JACKMANII'

'W. E. GLADSTONE'

CLEMATIS ALPINA 'FRANCES RIVIS'

PLANNING COLOUR COMBINATIONS

O NE OF THE MOST ATTRACTIVE WAYS to grow clematis in the garden is through other plants, mimicking how they twine through shrubs and trees in the wild. This technique provides infinite opportunities to play off their different habits, foliage, flower shapes and colours against those of other plants. Combining the flowers of clematis with the foliage of shrubs that have already bloomed is an effective way to extend both plants' season of interest.

CREATING CONTRASTS

You can usually find room for a clematis even in a fully-planted small garden – the rewards will be substantial in relation to the amount of planting space used. Use the opportunity to introduce flower colours that enhance the garden's vertical dimension.

Early-flowering clematis, such as alpinas and macropetalas, have abundant foliage which should be thinned to prevent it from smothering a host plant. Combining two clematis of the same species that have contrasting flower colours, such as C. macropetala 'Markham's Pink' with 'Blue Lagoon' or 'White Swan', is effective.

The early large-flowered hybrids bloom at the same time as ceanothus and roses (*see overleaf*). 'Guernsey Cream' has pale

> Golden foliage highlights purple flowers, and silver harmonizes with blue

cream flowers that would complement any blue ceanothus. Purple- and silver-leaved foliage shrubs are perfect foils for clematis, showing off not only the colour of the petals but their often prominent stamens.

Flowers in dusky and deep purple shades, such as those of C. viticella 'Mary Rose' or 'Royalty', are lost among dark green leaves. They will show up far better against golden foliage, such as that of Sambucus nigra 'Sutherland Gold' or Philadelphus coronarius 'Aureus'.

MIXING COOL COLOURS
The flowers of Clematis montana *and* Wisteria sinensis *create a harmonious blue and white display that is ideal for covering a strong pergola.*

▲ LIGHT AGAINST DARK
The purple-leaved Cotinus
coggygria *is an ideal foil
for the white clematis*
C. potaninii.

◀ GOLDEN LEAVES
The foliage of Choisya ternata
*'Sundance' enlivens the purple
flowers of* Clematis viticella.

CLEMATIS IN THE BORDER

Most of the mid-season and late-flowering clematis can be grown through herbaceous plants in the border without overwhelming them. Hybrids, such as 'The President', 'Madame Julia Correvon' and 'Duchess of Albany' (texensis group), can be pegged out and trained through plantings of phlox, artemisia, catmint, asters, fuchsias or even grasses. There are many possible colour combinations, from the subtle to the startling – such as red- and white-striped 'Dr Ruppel' with the variegated phlox 'Norah Leigh'. You could also allow climbing clematis to trail through herbaceous species such as C. *integrifolia*.

RECOMMENDED COMBINATIONS

CLEMATIS AND PARTNER	EFFECT
'Asao' with the large shrub *Cotinus coggygria* 'Royal Purple'.	Abundant, large, deep pink flowers in early summer blend with the shrub's purple foliage.
'Ernest Markham' with *Berberis thunbergii* f. *atropurpurea*.	Red clematis flowers glow among the small purple leaves of the berberis from mid-summer.
'Gipsy Queen' with *Helictotrichon sempervirens* (perennial evergreen grass).	From mid- to late summer, violet flowers thread between the blue-grey grass spikes.
'Etoile Violette' with *Pyrus salicifolia* 'Pendula', the weeping ornamental pear.	Masses of purple flowers stand out against silver foliage from late summer to autumn.
'Gravetye Beauty' with *Caryopteris* × *clandonensis* 'Heavenly Blue'.	In late summer, deep red flowers mingle with the soft blue blooms of the caryopteris.
Clematis × *durandii* with *Tropaeolum polyphyllum* (trailing perennial nasturtium).	Yellow flowers of the tropaeolum contrast with the indigo-blue clematis blooms.

COMBINING CLEMATIS WITH ROSES

M OST SHRUB AND CLIMBING ROSES are remarkably similar to many clematis in their cultivation requirements and flowering season. In addition, their size, shape and sturdy, branching structure make them ideal supports for clematis. There are plenty of rose types to choose as hosts, from ramblers that can reach 3–10m, often with clusters of small pale flowers, to the large-flowered modern hybrids with their extensive colour range.

PLANNING PLANT PARTNERS

The regular feeding and, if necessary, watering that enhances the flowering of roses will benefit clematis as well. You can also plan partnerships to make sure that the pruning times of both plants will coincide. Aim to avoid combining those clematis and roses that are prone to powdery mildew as this is likely to spread from one plant to the other. *Clematis crispa*

STRONG CONTRASTS
'Buff Beauty' rose supports 'Jackmanii Rubra', which has semi-double, pink flowers. The hybrid musk shrub roses are ideal hosts.

and the texensis types are particularly susceptible to mildew. The early-flowering alpinas and macropetalas all have very dense growth, and are ideal for training up and masking the usually bare lower stems of tall rambling and climbing roses. These clematis are less suitable for growing with small shrub roses, unless their bushy growth is thinned regularly. Clematis that flower earlier in the year and do not usually need pruning will benefit from thinning in late winter or early spring to five or six shoots which can be tied to the rose bush. This will avoid the dense tangle that can result if they are left unpruned. As

▲ SUBTLE BLENDS
*The rosy lilac blooms of
'Hagley Hybrid' appear to
give a second flowering to its
host, Rosa glauca.*

◄ PASTEL COMPANIONS
*The pale lavender-blue flowers
of 'Mrs Cholmondeley' nestle
among the glossy foliage
of the climbing rose 'New
Dawn', which has soft, shell-
pink blooms.*

with roses, the flowers will be fewer but often larger, better spaced and well formed.

All the large-flowered hybrids and the smaller-flowered viticellas that bloom in summer and early autumn are suitable for growing through roses. The early large-flowered hybrids bloom at the same time as most roses, from early to mid-summer, so that planning colour combinations can be

Late large-flowered hybrids and viticellas are ideal with old roses

very rewarding. Think about the effect you want to achieve: you may prefer a cool blend of pale or subtle shades or perhaps a contrasting scheme of vivid blooms.

The old-fashioned and species roses have few or no flowers by late summer, and are ideal hosts for some clematis, including the late large-flowered hybrids and Jackmaniis, and particularly the smaller-flowered

viticella hybrids. These have the advantage of being pruned hard every spring so that the roses can flower in early summer unencumbered. It is best to thin out their shoots as they regrow, and space them evenly around the rose, or they tend to form bundles of shoots that sit lopsidedly on the rose, become overcrowded and partially conceal the rose flowers.

GOOD COMBINATIONS

'Margot Koster', which has deep rosy-pink flowers, with the violet-lilac blooms of the rambling rose 'Veilchenblau'.

The silver-grey flowers of 'Silver Moon' with the purple-pink rose 'Gertrude Jekyll'.

'Corona', which has pink flowers tinged purple-red, with the hybrid perpetual rose 'Reine des Violettes'.

The white flowers of 'Gillian Blades' (*see p.58*) with the pink species rose Rosa × richardii.

Violet-flowered 'Royalty' with the egg-yolk yellow blooms of the rose 'Alister Stella Gray'.

The all-white combination of 'Marie Boisselot' and the rose 'Climbing Iceberg'.

CLEMATIS IN THE BORDER

To PROVIDE IMPACT IN A BORDER PLANTING, clematis can surpass many shrubs and perennials. Choose from the range of herbaceous types, the early-flowering hybrids that can be grown on tripods within the border and the late-flowering hybrids that will trail through mixed plantings. Although clematis are often added to existing border schemes, it is better to plan for their inclusion and to plant them in their own space rather than tucking them in as an afterthought.

HERBACEOUS CLEMATIS

The easiest clematis to include as part of a border planting are the herbaceous types, with compact growth that is more or less self-supporting compared with the climbers. These include quite bushy plants, such as *Clematis heracleifolia* and its cultivars. Thriving in sun or partial shade, they will reward you with bluish, fragrant flowers that sit above bunches of large, vine-like leaves. Other herbaceous varieties, such as *C. recta* 'Purpurea' and *C. integrifolia*, require support from twigs, canes, plant-rings or sturdy neighbouring plants. They are suitable for growing by retaining walls or banks that can be partially concealed by attractive swathes of draping stems.

There are also clematis that make good ground cover. *Clematis × jouiniana*, for example, can cover an area of up to 4m across and, when cut back in winter, leaves a large open space that is ideal for a spring bulb display. These can grow, bloom and die back before the clematis spreads out again.

COOL BLUES
The violet-blue flowers of Clematis × durandii *add depth of colour as they weave through a border planting of catmint* (Nepeta sibirica) *and goat's rue* (Galega).
C. × durandii *is an attractive, semi-herbaceous clematis plant that requires support from twigs or neighbouring plants.*

◄ ATTRACT WILDLIFE
In late summer, this combination of Clematis heracleifolia *var.* davidiana *and* Sedum *'Autumn Joy' will serve to attract butterflies and bees.*

▼ PURE WHITES
The small white flowers of Clematis flammula *combine effectively with those of* Lychnis coronaria *'Alba'. Both plants thrive in drier parts of the garden.*

CONSIDERING ALL THE OPTIONS

The early large-flowered hybrids are more tricky to grow among herbaceous plants, although they can be easily trained through shrubs. Alternatively, grow them over tripods placed within herbaceous plantings, to give borders a spectacular vertical accent.

The viticellas, texensis and the Jackmaniis can be grown on supports or allowed to scramble freely to add interest to virtually any late-flowering scheme. Easy to grow, they need pruning hard in late winter or

> Training a large-flowered hybrid over a tripod adds height to a border

early spring, at the same time as most herbaceous perennials. Where they are to trail through other plants, it is important to thin and space out the new shoots as they grow, pegging them down into the soil (*see p.33*) or just threading them through neighbouring plants, otherwise clumps of shoots can smother host plants. Most strong-growing herbaceous plants, such as phlox or asters, however, can support the weight of a clematis shoot or two.

CHOOSING HOST TREES AND SHRUBS

TREES AND SHRUBS MAKE USEFUL PARTNERS for clematis, which use them as a frame to twine around as they grow upwards to reach the light. In their flowering season clematis provide colour and interest, perhaps decorating a bare trunk or forming a canopy over branches or arching stems. There are few sights as beautiful in the garden as a large tree draped in the white or pale pink flowers of a *Clematis montana*. Some species, such as *C. vitalba*, can cover their host entirely.

ESTABLISHING HEALTHY PLANTS

When using a tree or a shrub as a host plant, make sure that its root system is not competing with the clematis for water and nutrients. To do this, plant the clematis away from the base of the host and mulch with well-rotted manure each spring. Consider the size of the host plant in relation to the vigour of the clematis. A shrub or small tree needs to be able to bear the weight of the clematis and not be smothered by it.

Avoid planting clematis near trees with dense root systems, such as beech and cherry. Old conifers that have dry soil under their canopies can be used to provide support if the clematis is planted about 1–2m outside the "drip line" (the edge of the canopy and the rain shadow it casts). The clematis can be trained over the ground, along a length of rope or up a cane to reach the tree.

▲ COVERING A BARE TREE TRUNK
Clematis alpina *combines well with small trees, although it requires help to reach the lower branches. Canes or twine used for training the stems will soon be covered by growth.*

◄ AN EFFECTIVE FOLIAGE BACKDROP
Clematis can be used to enliven a shrub that has already flowered, such as in this planting of 'Cardinal Wyszynski' *with the rhododendron* 'Goldsworth Yellow'.

A LONG SHOW
Lilac can act as the perfect host for clematis. In this planting, a combination of two hybrid clematis will bloom in summer after the lilac has finished flowering. 'Fireworks' can grow up to 3m high into the shrub, while 'Lady Northcliffe' clambers around the lower branches.

PLANNING PERFECT PARTNERSHIPS

Almost all the large-flowered hybrids, viticellas and compact species clematis make good partners for established shrubs that reach 2–5m. The alpinas and macropetalas are best for growing among small trees that have low, forking branches, such as maple or magnolia.

To scramble over large, mature trees, choose *C. montana* for spring and early summer flowers, and *C. potaninii* or 'Paul Farges' for small, white flowers in late summer and autumn. Alternatively, *C. tangutica* and 'Bill MacKenzie', with yellow bells in late summer and autumn, can reach 5–7m in height. Many of the montanas grow to 8m or more, so be sure that the tree is large enough not be too overwhelmed by such a vigorous clematis. It is difficult to get access to prune tangled, over-dense growth once it is scrambling high through the branches of a tall tree.

When planting a clematis with a shrub, consider the flowering time of each plant, how they will complement one another and any pruning methods involved. Late summer- and autumn-flowering clematis need hard pruning but the lower stems attached to the tree or shrub can often be left unpruned to give the new shoots a head start each year.

GOOD HOSTS FOR CLEMATIS

TREES

Acer tataricum subsp. *ginnala*
Catalpa bignonioides 'Aurea'
Chamaecyparis, such as *C. lawsoniana* 'Pembury Blue'
Magnolia x *soulangeana*
Crab apple, such as *Malus* x *zumi* 'Golden Hornet'
Pine, such as *Pinus sylvestris*
Weeping pear (*Pyrus salicifolia* 'Pendula')
Sorbus, such as *S. aucuparia* group
Yew, such as *Taxus baccata* 'Fastigiata'
Thuja, such as *T. plicata*

SHRUBS

Berberis, such as *B. thunbergii*
Buddleja, such as *B. alternifolia* 'Argentea'
Ceanothus, such as *C.* 'Cascade'
Cotinus, such as *C. coggygria* 'Royal Purple'
Heather, such as *Erica carnea* 'Springwood White'
Hydrangea aspera **Villosa Group**
Juniper, such as *Juniperus* 'Pfitzeriana Aurea'
Lilac (*Syringa*), such as 'Madame Lemoine'
Philadelphus, such as *P.* 'Belle Etoile'
Rhododendron, such as *R.* 'Sappho'

COVERING VERTICAL SURFACES

CLEMATIS GROWING ON WALLS, fences, trellis and obelisks are a familiar and attractive sight. With the exception of roses, there are few plants that can match clematis in beauty and usefulness for clothing vertical surfaces. Most clematis are reasonably lightweight in their growth and climb easily, their leaf tendrils needing to gain only a little purchase from a few vine eyes threaded with garden twine or wire to reach the top of a wall.

SUPPORTING CLEMATIS

For dense cover, there are many types of mesh-like materials available as supports, from very lightweight plastic netting to wooden trellis. However, other climbing plants, particularly roses, make equally good supports. The foliage of some clematis, particularly the early-flowering hybrids, can begin to look rather tatty by the end of the summer. Growing them through other plants can disguise or even conceal this disappointing trait.

Some clematis do have fine foliage, especially the evergreen *Clematis armandii*, which needs plenty of shelter to protect its glossy, leathery leaves. Likewise, *C. cirrhosa*, the winter-flowering clematis, and its variations have attractive, finely cut foliage and are best appreciated growing over an arch or arbour so that you can enjoy looking up into the freckled bells.

▲ OVER A PILLAR
Two of the most reliable and popular clematis, the stripy-flowered 'Nelly Moser' and 'The President', conceal a brick pillar with the aid of strands of wire.

◄ SHELTERED SITE
Clematis armandii *'Apple Blossom' needs the protection of a sheltered wall to produce its clusters of white flowers offset by glossy foliage.*

C. *montana* has fine purple-leaved forms, such as 'Warwickshire Rose', and can reach 10m. Its dense growth and vigour make it useful for covering unsightly buildings.

For very cold, exposed walls and fences up to 2–3m high, the best choices are the alpinas and macropetalas. These are valuable for their fresh foliage, spring flowers and fluffy seedheads in summer.

Early large-flowered hybrids, such as 'Marie Boisselot', often have very lanky growth and bloom only at the top. It is

▲ MAXIMUM COVERAGE
Clematis montana *is a vigorous species that is capable of weaving through and over fences and covering unsightly buildings. In late spring it bursts into flower.*

▼ OBELISK OF COLOUR
'Etoile Violette' and the sweet pea 'Noel Sutton' (an annual) are both vigorous plants that grow quickly to cover a wooden obelisk, putting on a colourful late summer show.

> ## A montana makes fine camouflage for an ugly building or wall

often worth spiralling the shoots of these clematis around tripods or obelisks to encourage them to produce flowers more evenly over the plant. This technique does not work so well for late-flowering hybrids, which have much more vigorous growth. Their shoots tend to leap up vertically at so fast a rate as to defy training. Instead, combine them with other climbing plants, such as honeysuckle or roses, so that they can clamber freely.

GROWING CLEMATIS IN CONTAINERS

CLEMATIS ARE EASY TO GROW IN CONTAINERS, allowing their beauty to be enjoyed on patios, balconies and terraces. Only the most vigorous, such as the montanas, are really impractical for container-growing. Any style of pot or planter you choose can be combined with a climbing plant support, from the wide range of tripods, obelisks and woven willow cones to intricate wire spheres. (To make your own wire globe, *see pages 36–37*.)

CONSIDERING PRACTICALITIES

The more vigorous the clematis, the bigger the container you will need; even with some of the newer, very compact clematis, always make sure that containers are at least 45cm deep and wide. It is best to fill them with a loam-based compost blended with some slow-release fertilizer. Regular watering will be essential, but covering the compost with a pebble or cocoa-shell mulch will help to conserve moisture.

Planting a two-year-old clematis with a well-developed root system in a large pot will give you a good display in the first year. Every following year, scrape away the top 10cm of compost, being careful not to damage the roots of the plant, and replace with fresh compost. To encourage the most flowers, feed the clematis throughout the

▲ PYRAMID OF EXOTIC BLOOMS
A slightly tender Clematis florida 'Sieboldii' grows well in containers, its eye-catching flowers shown to great effect.

◄ AN EXUBERANT DISPLAY
To get value from a container display, choose a reliable clematis with a long flowering period such as 'Comtesse de Bouchaud'.

growing season with a liquid seaweed fertilizer or a tomato-growing formula.

Choose clematis that will give maximum value in terms of display. 'Arabella', for example, has a very long flowering season and grows to only 1–2m; 'Niobe' is also a good choice because it can be encouraged

---

During the summer, containers may need watering every day

---

with light pruning to give a prolonged flowering. Combining one early- and one late-flowering clematis gives a long display, but you will need to take extra care when pruning. Alternatively, planting two clematis with the same flowering season allows you to create attractive colour combinations.

GOOD CHOICES

Alpinas (*see pp.50–51*)
Macropetalas (*see pp.50–51*)
Viticellas (*see pp.66–67*)
Clematis florida 'Flore Pleno' Double white
'Barbara Dibley' Purple-red, deeper midribs
'Beauty of Worcester' Intense blue
'Bees' Jubilee' (*see p.57*) Pink with deeper bars
'Carnaby' (*see p.57*) Deep pink
'Comtesse de Bouchaud' (*see p.62*) Pink
'Countess of Lovelace' (*see p.61*) Lilac-blue
'Elsa Späth' (*see p.54*) Deep blue
'H. F. Young' (*see p.54*) Mid-blue
'Hagley Hybrid' (*see p.62*) Pale mauve-pink
'John Huxtable' Violet-blue flowers
'Miss Bateman' (*see p.58*) White
'Mrs George Jackman' (*see p.61*) White
'Niobe' (*see p.59*) Ruby red
'Perle d'Azur' (*see p.8*) Clear blue flowers
'Proteus' (*see p.61*) Mauve-pink

▲ ALPINE CLEMATIS
A tender, evergreen clematis from New Zealand, C. × cartmanii 'Joe' needs to be kept dry and protected in winter. Grown in a pot, it can be moved easily.

◀ A FOCAL POINT
Clematis macropetala *'Maidwell Hall' cascades from an urn. Its stems are trained over netting that has been draped over the sides of the urn.*

CARING FOR YOUR CLEMATIS

PRIOR TO PLANTING

WITH SO MANY LOVELY CLEMATIS now available at almost every garden centre, it can be hard to resist buying on impulse. But it's important to be sure what type of clematis it is, so that you know when it's going to flower, and to which pruning group it belongs. Try always to have a site in mind, to know how your clematis will be supported and to have supports ready in place.

SELECTING THE BEST PLANTS

Two-year-old clematis, like the one on the right, are by far the easiest to establish in the garden and, for the speed at which they will grow away, are well worth paying a little more for. Look out for plants that have more than one stem growing from the base, and healthy foliage. Roots should be sufficiently developed for you to see them through the holes in the base of the pot, but not growing out of the holes and into the display bed. Clematis are unwieldy to transport: take care of the plant's fragile stems, and do not remove any protective cane caps until you have finished planting.

A PROMISING PLANT
Look carefully before you decide whether to buy – height is not as important as the number and vigour of the plant's shoots. It need not have flower buds, though two-year-old plants may have plenty.

Foliage should cover the whole plant

Look for a number of growing shoots

The roots should be strong and healthy

BUYING TIPS

• Although container-grown clematis can be planted all season, don't buy and plant them during hot spells when the soil is dry.

• The huge popularity of clematis means that suppliers restock frequently, so don't accept a bad plant; wait for new ones to be delivered or ask if you can place an order.

• If you can't find a particular clematis, consider mail-order specialists; ask them what age the plant they dispatch will be.

◄ GRAND FINALE *Enchanting autumn seedheads follow* Clematis tibetana's *yellow bells.*

PUTTING UP TRELLIS

MOST CLEMATIS NEED THIN SUPPORTS such as wires or battens to twine around. Trellising is a simple and lasting solution for wall-training. The method below enables you to lower the trellis with the clematis clinging onto it, should you need to reach the wall for maintenance. Use the brick courses as a guide to ensure that the trellis is (or at least looks!) straight. There are ready-to-assemble packs of trellis strips to hide drainpipes, if you wish.

FIXING TRELLIS TO A WALL

YOU NEED:

MATERIALS
• Trellis panel
• 2 pieces of 3.5×2.5cm batten, the width of the panel in length
• 6 size 8, 50mm (2in) screws
• Rawlplugs
• 2 hinges, plus screws
• 2 hooks and eyes

TOOLS
• Pencil
• Metal tape measure
• Drill (preferably electric) with wood and masonry bits
• Hammer
• Bradawl
• Screwdriver

1 **Hold** the trellis panel in position against the wall. Align the edges with the straight lines of the brickwork. Mark the position of the trellis panel at the top and lower edges, and on each side.

2 **Drill** 3 holes in each piece of batten, one at each end and one in the centre, ready for screwing to the wall. Drill onto a spare offcut of wood, placed beneath the batten.

3 **Hold** the battens against the wall, aligning the edges with the positional marks for the trellis.

4 **Mark the position** of the screwholes on the wall, before removing the battens. Drill holes in the wall (*see inset*), then hammer in the rawlplugs.

5 **Screw the top** batten securely to the wall, first checking again that its upper edge aligns with the positional marks for the trellis.

6 **Screw the hinges** onto the lower edge of the bottom batten, having started the holes using a bradawl. Position the batten to align with the positional marks for the trellis and screw securely to the wall.

7 **Hold the base** of the trellis panel alongside the lower batten, aligning the ends. Screw the hinges attached to the batten to the bottom of the trellis panel (*see above*). You may need to support the trellis panel to do this.

8 **Raise the trellis** into position to check that it aligns with the top batten. Then screw hooks into each end of the top batten and eyes into each end of the trellis panel (*see inset*) in order to hold it in place.

FIXING A TRELLIS KIT TO A DRAINPIPE

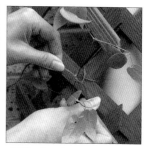

1 **Lay out** the 3 strips of trellis from the pack, interlocking the edges of the lattice. Fasten them together temporarily with rubber bands.

2 **Position the trellis** around the drainpipe and fasten in place with the clips provided in the pack. Remove the rubber bands.

3 **Tie the clematis** shoots onto the trellis with soft twine. Use figure-of-eight knots to allow the stem to expand and move slightly.

PLANTING AND WATERING

THE BEST TIMES TO PLANT CLEMATIS are autumn or early spring, although any time of year is possible as long as you water frequently in the first summer. Incorporate a watering system (*see opposite*) at the planting stage. Although most clematis need light and some sun to flower well, their roots like to be kept cool. A mulch helps to shade the roots and to conserve moisture. Clematis prefer well-drained soil and need plentiful feeding and watering until established.

PLANTING CLEMATIS BY A WALL OR FENCE

When planting a clematis against a wall, position it well away from the base (up to 30cm), especially where there is overhang from gutters or other structures. The soil under a wall is generally very dry. Dig a deep hole so that, once planted, the first 10–20cm of the clematis stems are below the soil surface. Deep planting encourages new shoots to develop at the base should you have to cut the clematis right back.

If the soil is heavy, improve the drainage by working some fine grit or sharp sand into the soil at the base of the planting hole. Mix in plenty of well-rotted manure or garden compost and some bonemeal (wear gloves when handling) with the soil, especially at the bottom of the hole. Water well and mulch the surface. It is best not to use chipped bark as a mulch because it can harbour pests.

SHADING PLANT ROOTS
• A mulch of well-rotted manure or leaf-mould looks best in a border or with shrubs.
• A pebble or gravel mulch is ideal by a wall.
• Low-growing plants growing in front of the clematis will shield the roots from the sun.

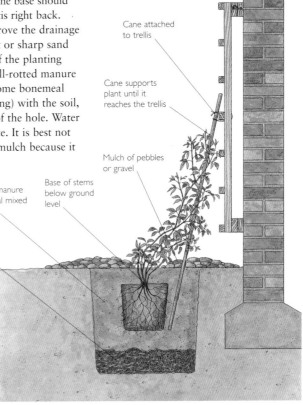

Cane attached to trellis

Cane supports plant until it reaches the trellis

Mulch of pebbles or gravel

Base of stems below ground level

Well-rotted manure and bonemeal mixed with the soil

Well-rotted manure improves soil structure and encourages deep rooting

PLANTING DEEPLY
Plant clematis deeply, enriching the soil with damp, well-rotted manure or garden compost. Mulching around the base of the plant shades the roots and conserves moisture.

PLANTING A CLEMATIS TO GROW INTO A SHRUB

Plant the clematis away from its host so that there is less competition for food and moisture. The clematis needs to be outside the rainshadow and drip line created by the shrub. If the shrub is not fully grown, you must take its eventual spread into account; a vigorous clematis can easily travel up to 2m, if necessary, before reaching its host.

1 **Dig a generous hole** at least 45cm wide and deep. Mix well-rotted manure or garden compost into the soil.

2 **Mark** the ground level with a horizontal cane. Put in the clematis, checking that at least 10cm of stem is buried.

3 **Mulch** the area with well-rotted manure or compost after watering in. Lean the cane towards the shrub.

WATERING CLEMATIS

Most clematis need plenty of moisture in order to thrive. This is particularly important while the plant is getting established. To make watering as efficient as possible, it is a good idea to bury a piece of pipe or a flower pot alongside the clematis at planting time; pouring the water into it will ensure that it reaches the plant's roots. Simply watering around the base of the plant can encourage roots to form near the soil surface, making the plant more likely to suffer from drought. Once a mulch has been laid it is, in any case, difficult for water to penetrate the ground and in hot weather a lot can be lost through evaporation.

Once established, a clematis should flourish without watering if the soil has been enriched with organic matter (such as rotted manure), encouraging good, deep root growth. Renew mulches as necessary.

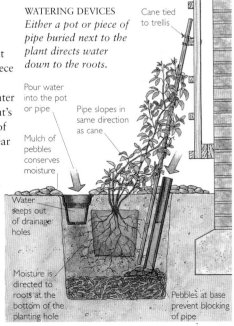

WATERING DEVICES
Either a pot or piece of pipe buried next to the plant directs water down to the roots.

Cane tied to trellis

Pour water into the pot or pipe

Pipe slopes in same direction as cane

Mulch of pebbles conserves moisture

Water seeps out of drainage holes

Moisture is directed to roots at the bottom of the planting hole

Pebbles at base prevent blocking of pipe

TRAINING CLEMATIS

EXCEPT FOR THE HERBACEOUS TYPES, clematis naturally twine readily around the stems of a host plant or other support. This may make training seem unnecessary. However, most flower better and more profusely if trained in some way, with their stems spread evenly over a trellis or shrub, or pegged along the ground. If left to themselves, plants tend to become tangled, resulting in smaller and fewer flowers that are partly obscured by crowded foliage.

TYING IN CLEMATIS STEMS

Initially, it is best to tie the stems of a newly planted clematis to its support, then it will start to attach itself using its twining leaf stalks. Use garden twine or twist ties, but take care, as the stems are very fragile. Plants flower more evenly if the main stems can be trained horizontally at first, or spiralled around a pillar or obelisk. Late-flowering hybrids grow too quickly to make it worth trying to train in this way.

IDEAS FOR SUPPORTS

• Vertical wires stretched between eyes screwed into a wall or the pillars of a pergola, or wide-gauge wire netting (ask for sheep or pig wire), are less obtrusive than trellis.
• Metal obelisks, often supplied complete with wire panels for better coverage.
• Hazel or willow wigwams, bought ready-made or constructed from pliable stems.

▲ THE TWINING HABIT OF CLEMATIS
Clematis cling by twining their leaf stalks around wires, strings or stems of host plants. You just need to encourage the natural process.

▶ USING FIGURE-OF-EIGHT KNOTS
When tying with string, take care with the brittle stems and use loose figure-of-eight knots to prevent them chafing against the support.

PEGGING OUT A CLEMATIS IN THE BORDER

Late-flowering clematis, especially the texensis and viticella hybrids, can look good grown along the ground in borders or beds. Here they spread out, twining through the stems of shrubs and herbaceous plants or forming attractive, light ground cover. It is important to direct these clematis, pegging them out where you want them to flower. If left untrained, their stems tend to form a tight tangle and create a far less elegant display, with flowers partially lost among the foliage. The technique involved is very straightforward. All you need to pin the stems along the ground are some 15–18cm lengths of wire bent into hooks (*right*).

WIRE HOOKS

WHEN TO START PEGGING OUT
The new growth of Clematis viticella *tends to leap up in a confused tangle in spring. When the growth is about 50cm–1m long, it is time to start training it outwards.*

1 **Pull the stems** apart gently, selecting about a third of them to peg out. Do not worry if some shoots break in the process. Cut the remainder close to the ground.

2 **Using the wire hooks,** peg out the stems around the plant, inserting a hook every 50cm or so. You can encourage the growth in any direction you wish.

3 **Train the stems** once again as they grow, then leave the clematis to its own devices. By mid- to late summer, a well-established, vigorous plant like this will cover an area of about 4–5m in blooms. New shoots will also emerge from the centre of the plant to flower later in the season.

LOOKING AFTER CLEMATIS

IF CLEMATIS ARE GIVEN A GOOD START by thorough preparation at the planting stage, they will not demand a great deal of time and attention in later years. Feed and water plants generously in their first season, but, once established, they will need little more than a good mulch of rotted manure each spring. Even pruning (see pp.38–43) is not essential for every type of clematis.

AT A GLANCE		WHAT TO DO
SPRING	• Prune • Feed plants • Renew mulches	Prune (see pp.38–43) to encourage healthy growth and more flowers. Mulch with well-rotted cow or horse manure to feed plants and conserve moisture. Where pebble or gravel mulches have been laid, use pelleted chicken manure or liquid seaweed fertilizer. Renew stone mulches if necessary as they help to conserve moisture, shade roots and keep down weeds.
SUMMER	• Feed plants in containers • Train new shoots • Water young plants • Take cuttings	Feed clematis in pots with liquid seaweed or tomato fertilizer. This will also help clematis in the garden that are not thriving. Train new shoots to prevent them from becoming tangled and to spread growth evenly over a host or support. Water young plants until they are established. Before mid-summer, take cuttings (see pp.44–45) of clematis you wish to propagate.
AUTUMN	• Collect seed • Hard-prune Group 3 clematis if required	Gather seedheads (see pp.46–47) for sowing. If the brown stems of a Group 3 clematis mar the attractiveness of a host shrub in winter, the stems can be safely cut hard back (see p.43) once they have died down; otherwise, wait until spring.
WINTER	• Protect tender clematis against frost	Cover tender clematis with straw or thick, small-mesh netting. Move plants in containers into a greenhouse or conservatory.

GUARDING AGAINST PESTS

Good general care of plants helps to promote their health and make them less likely to succumb to pests. There are also preventative measures that will deter the pests most often associated with clematis –

EARWIG DAMAGE
Earwigs take notches out of the sides of flowers and leaves. Good garden hygiene will discourage them from living under old vegetation.

slugs, mice, earwigs and aphids. Slugs are the most common pests – they damage new shoots, sometimes surprisingly high up on plants. Discourage them by placing sharp grit around the base of the plant or use beer traps. Also remove garden debris and old hollow stems that can harbour both slugs and earwigs.

Mice can chew away plants as they grow. The plants usually recover but not until a whole season later. Covering young shoots with chicken wire will act as a deterrent. You can pinch off shoots badly infested by aphids or spray with insecticidal soap.

KEEPING CLEMATIS HEALTHY

Healthy, vigorous plants are much more resistant to disease. Bear in mind, too, that correct pruning not only helps to promote better flowering but also includes cutting out dead and damaged wood, thus improving air circulation and removing potential entry points for infection.

Many clematis, especially the early- and late-flowering species and the viticella hybrids, are virtually trouble-free. However, over-breeding of the large-flowered hybrids has meant that some have become liable to clematis wilt, and others to mildew.

Clematis wilt looks disastrous but the plant may be saved. Cut out all affected stems, if necessary right down to the ground, and feed the plant with liquid seaweed fertilizer. If the clematis is planted deeply (*see p.30*), it may re-shoot from below ground.

Mildew is best discouraged by good air circulation. Do not train clematis prone to mildew flat against walls or among roses. Slime flux is a rare disease that usually affects only *Clematis montana*. Prune and destroy the affected wood. If the plant dies, do not replant a clematis in the same spot.

CLEMATIS WILT
The first sign of this disease is the wilting of some shoots or even the entire plant. It most often occurs in early summer when the plant is full of young growth and flower buds. The diseased shoots turn brown and collapse.

SLIME FLUX
This disease is rare, but can be fatal; it causes a slimy, sap-like substance to ooze thickly from the stems near the base of the plant.

MILDEW ON CLEMATIS
Texensis hybrids and closely related species, such as Clematis addisonii and C. reticulata, are prone to this greyish fungal infection.

A CLEMATIS GLOBE

THE TWINING HABIT of clematis can be utilized to create architectural shapes over supporting wire structures. A wire globe clothed in a clematis makes a simple but very striking feature. The technique is easy, with new shoots being trained in as the clematis grows to obscure the wire. In the flowering season, you will be rewarded by a sphere of blooms and, with some clematis, a second flush later in the year.

MAKING A WIRE GLOBE

1 **Insert 3 canes** firmly into the compost, spacing them evenly around the clematis. Tie them at the top with wire to form a wigwam.

Position canes near the edge of the container

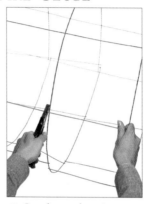

2 **Cut the mesh** to form 6 ladder-like strips 140cm long. Cut each with 2 prongs at both ends for fixing into the compost and to the canes.

YOU NEED:

MATERIALS
• Clematis potted in a container, approximately 45cm in diameter. Choose a compact type of clematis (*see pp.24–25*) and plant it attached to the support it came with
• 3 bamboo canes, approximately 1m long
• Wide-gauge (20cm mesh) galvanized wire netting, 220×140cm

TOOLS
• Pliers or pincers for cutting wire

3 **Bend the prongs** at the bottom of the first wire strip inwards, and insert them securely into the compost at the edge of the container. Form the strip into a semi-circular shape.

4 **Shape the wire ends** at the top of the strip into hooks that will fit around the tops of the canes. Twist the ends together to hold the wire securely on the canes.

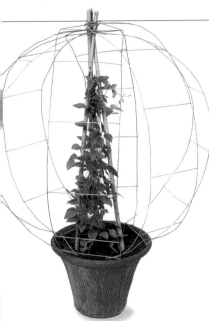

5 **Complete the wire globe** by fixing the remaining 5 wire strips in the same way, spacing them evenly around the edges of the container to form a balloon shape.

6 **Detach and thread the stems** through to the outside along the base of the globe. Start weaving them in and out of the wires. Continue to direct the stems as they grow.

A SPHERE OF FLOWERS
Clematis florida *'Flore Pleno'* conceals the frame beneath abundant double white flowers. Initially, take the stems in a horizontal or diagonal direction, to encourage the clematis to produce flowers on the bottom half of the globe as well as the top.

PRACTICAL TIPS

• Clematis that are slightly tender, such as C. *florida* 'Flore Pleno', may need to be moved into a greenhouse or conservatory for protection in winter.
• In spring, scrape away the top compost and apply a fresh layer. Add some pellets of slow-release fertilizer.
• Prune the clematis according to its group and train new stems around the globe as they grow.

PRUNING CLEMATIS

CLEMATIS VARY IN THEIR FLOWERING TIMES and differ in their pruning requirements. They are generally divided into three main pruning groups. Clematis that flower in spring require no pruning (Pruning Group 1), those that flower in early summer require light pruning (Pruning Group 2) and those that flower from mid-summer onwards require hard pruning (Pruning Group 3). The following pages list clematis in each group and show how to prune them.

FLOWERING TIME AND PRUNING

The way in which the different clematis are pruned relates to the age of wood on which they bear their flowers.

PRUNING GROUP 1 clematis flower in spring on stems that grew and ripened in the previous year, so any pruning removes potential flowering wood. Therefore, they are only pruned to thin them when really necessary – which makes them great for covering eyesores year-round, or training into less accessible places where regular access would be inconvenient.

PRUNING GROUP 2 includes all the large-flowered hybrids that bloom in early summer. Their flowers are borne on sideshoots that grow from the previous year's ripened stems. As with Group 1, therefore, they must not be hard-pruned if flowers are to form – but light pruning will stimulate more flowering sideshoots on the stems that remain. They should be sited and trained so that you can gain access to the stems to prune lightly in late winter.

PRUNING GROUP 3, the mid-season to late-flowering clematis, are the easiest for gardeners who hate making pruning decisions – you simply cut the lot back in late winter or early spring. Strong new stems will then grow vigorously and bear flowers all in a single season.

WHEN TO PRUNE CLEMATIS

PRUNING GROUP 1

Prune only to thin if necessary, in late winter or after flowering (see p.40). The following can also be hard-pruned after flowering:

Alpinas
Macropetalas
Clematis barbellata
Clematis cirrhosa
Clematis koreana
Clematis 'Pruinina'

Never cut these clematis hard back into old, dark wood:

Montanas
Clematis armandii
Clematis chrysocoma
Clematis gracilifolia
Clematis × vedrariensis

PRUNING GROUP 2

Prune lightly in late winter to strong growth and buds, leaving a good framework (see p.41). This group includes all the early large-flowered hybrids, singles and doubles.

'MISS BATEMAN'

PRUNING GROUP 3

Prune hard in late winter/early spring, cutting all stems back (see p.43). This group includes all the late large-flowered hybrids, the mid- to late-flowering species and herbaceous clematis.

'BILL MACKENZIE'

How to Prune Clematis Stems

Always use sharp secateurs when pruning, and position cuts a few millimetres above a leaf joint (node), taking care not to damage any new buds or shoots sprouting from it if growth has already begun. If you have a choice of where to prune to, as on the early large-flowered hybrids, choose a really strong-looking bud or shoot. When pruning out old unproductive growth, make the cut close to a branching point. Alternatively, prune to the ground to encourage new growth from below the soil.

PRUNING OUT OLD GROWTH
Prune down to a branching point, leaving a bold framework. Make a clean cut without leaving snags.

LIGHT PRUNING
In late winter, prune directly above a pair of strong buds. The new spring shoots indicate the best place to prune.

HARD PRUNING
Cut immediately above the lowest pair of strong buds on each stem – this will be 15–30cm above soil level.

Renovating Clematis

If you take over an old garden there may be massive tangles of overgrown clematis to tidy up. Almost all clematis except the montanas and early large-flowered hybrids can be cut back to the ground, so if you don't know what you have inherited, the safest course is to renovate it as if it were one of these. Take the whole clematis off its host plant or trellis, if necessary, then remove almost all the old growth, and all the dense twigs and old seedheads. Retain 3–5 2m-long shoots to train back in place.

A NEGLECTED CLEMATIS   AFTER RENOVATION

AN OVERGROWN CLEMATIS
On the far left, an old large-flowered hybrid, unpruned for over three years, is a typical problem that you may have to tackle. It can be hard to know where to start, but be brave. Remove almost all the old growth, retaining only a few good long shoots. These may need fanning out slightly and retraining – here, they have been guided back into the branches of a conifer. The clematis should flower in the summer, helping you to identify it if necessary.

PRUNING GROUP 1

It is not essential to prune clematis in this group, but they do benefit from occasional thinning (*see below*), to reinvigorate them and to reduce their weight and bulk – particularly where they are grown to form swathes over arbours, gates and arches.

Most can also be cut back hard if necessary, except for *Clematis montana*, which dislikes hard pruning into old wood. To renovate montanas, you can cut away all the old, dense, twiggy growth, but always leave some strong stems intact.

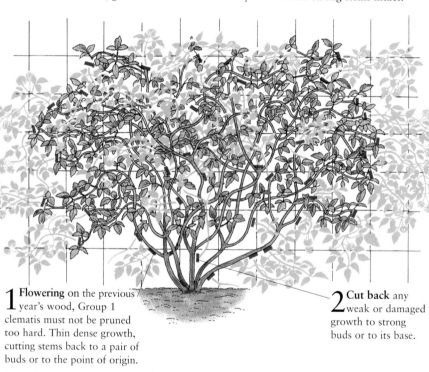

1 **Flowering** on the previous year's wood, Group 1 clematis must not be pruned too hard. Thin dense growth, cutting stems back to a pair of buds or to the point of origin.

2 **Cut back** any weak or damaged growth to strong buds or to its base.

CLEMATIS IN PRUNING GROUP 1

Clematis alpina
  'Columbine'
  'Constance'
  'Frances Rivis'
  'Frankie'
  'Helsingborg'
  'Pink Flamingo'
  'Rosy Pagoda'
  'Ruby'
  subsp. *sibirica*
  'White Moth'
  'Tage Lundell'
  'Willy'

Clematis armandii
  'Apple Blossom'
  'Snowdrift'
Clematis × *cartmanii*
  'Joe'
Clematis chrysocoma
Clematis cirrhosa
  var. *balearica*
  'Freckles'
  'Wisley Cream'
Clematis gracilifolia
Clematis indivisa
Clematis koreana
  f. *lutea*

Clematis macropetala
  'Blue Bird'
  'Jan Lindmark'
  'Lagoon' (syn. 'Blue Lagoon')
  'Maidwell Hall'
  'Markham's Pink'
Clematis montana
  'Broughton Star'
  'Elizabeth'
  'Fragrant Spring'
  'Freda'
  f. *grandiflora*
  'Marjorie'

  'Mayleen'
  'Picton's Variety'
  var. *rubens*
  var. *sericea*
  'Tetrarose'
  'Warwickshire Rose'
  var. *wilsonii*
  'Pruinina'
  'Rosie O'Grady'
  'White Swan'

PRUNING GROUP 2

This group is composed entirely of the early large-flowered hybrids (*see overleaf*), including those with double flowers, whose second flush later in the summer produces only single blooms. Although Group 2 clematis can be left unpruned, the flowers are larger and foliage is healthier on well-pruned plants.

The clematis in this group require light pruning in late winter or early spring to thin the plant down to a framework of well-spaced one- or two-year-old stems. Prune out any weak growth and all the twiggy sideshoots. This will help to stimulate new shoots and encourage more prolific flowering. The fat leaf axil buds that appear in early spring produce the first batch of flowers.

You can prolong the flowering season of these clematis if you stagger the pruning by cutting back some shoots to healthy buds later than others (*see p.43*). There will not be as many flowers in the main flush as with the standard pruning procedure but the flowering period will be longer overall.

Avoid using a shrub such as buddleja, caryopteris or perovskia, which is cut hard back in spring, to support a Group 2 clematis. It will be nearly impossible to prune the shrub once the clematis has started twining through it.

Alternatively, Group 2 clematis can be grown with minimal pruning, cutting back hard every three or four years. The first flush of flowers is lost after hard pruning, but the second has larger, more plentiful blooms.

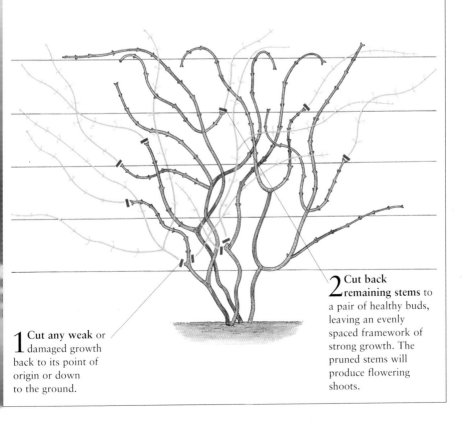

1 **Cut any weak** or damaged growth back to its point of origin or down to the ground.

2 **Cut back remaining stems** to a pair of healthy buds, leaving an evenly spaced framework of strong growth. The pruned stems will produce flowering shoots.

CLEMATIS IN PRUNING GROUP 2

Clematis patens	'Elsa Späth'	'Lady Northcliffe'	'Pôhjanael'
'Andromeda'	'Empress of India'	'Lasurstern'	'Prins Hendrik'
'Arctic Queen'	'Etoile de Malicorne'	'Liberation'	'Proteus'
'Asao'	'Etoile de Paris'	'Lincoln Star'	'Ramona'
'Barbara Dibley'	'Fair Rosamond'	'Lord Nevill'	'Richard Pennell'
'Barbara Jackman'	'Fairy Queen'	'Louise Rowe'	'Rouge Cardinal'
'Beauty of Richmond'	'Fireworks'	'Marcel Moser'	'Royal Velvet'
'Beauty of Worcester'	'Fuji-musume'	'Marie Boisselot'	'Royalty'
'Bees' Jubilee'	'Général Sikorski'	'Masquerade' (syn.	'Ruby Glow'
'Belle Nantaise'	'Gillian Blades'	'Maskarad')	'Scartho Gem'
'Belle of Woking'	'Glynderek'	'Maureen'	'Sealand Gem'
'Blue Ravine'	'Guernsey Cream'	'Miss Bateman'	'Serenata'
'Bracebridge Star'	'Haku-ôkan	'Miss Crawshay'	'Silver Moon'
'Burma Star'	'H.F. Young'	'Monte Cassino'	'Snow Queen'
'Chalcedony'	'Henryi'	'Moonlight'	'Sugar Candy'
'Cardinal Wyszynski'	'Horn of Plenty'	'Mrs Bush'	'Sunset'
'Carnaby'	'Jackmanii Alba'	'Mrs Cholmondeley'	'Sylvia Denny'
'Carnival Queen'	'Jackmanii Rubra'	'Mrs George Jackman'	'The President'
'Charissima'	'James Mason'	'Mrs Hope'	'The Vagabond'
'Corona'	'Joan Picton'	'Mrs James Mason'	'Twilight'
'Countess of Lovelace'	'John Paul II' (syn.	'Mrs N. Thompson'	'Wada's Primrose'
'Crimson King'	'Jan Pawel II')	'Mrs P. B. Truax'	'Warszawaska Nike'
'Daniel Deronda'	'John Warren'	'Mrs Spencer Castle'	'W. E. Gladstone'
'Dawn'	'Kathleen Dunford'	'Multi Blue'	'Will Goodwin'
'Doctor Ruppel'	'Kathleen Wheeler'	'Myôjô'	'William Kennett'
'Duchess of Edinburgh'	'Keith Richardson'	'Nelly Moser'	'Victoria'
'Duchess of Sutherland'	'Kiri Te Kanawa'	'Niobe'	'Vino'
'Edith'	'Lady Caroline Nevill'	'Peveril Pearl'	'Violet Elizabeth'
'Edouard Desfossé'	'Lady Londesborough'	'Pink Fantasy'	'Vyvyan Pennell'

CLEMATIS IN PRUNING GROUP 3

Clematis addisonii	*Clematis ladakhiana*	'Bill MacKenzie'	'Lady Bird Johnson'
Clematis aethusifolia	*Clematis potaninii*	'Black Prince'	'Madame Edouard
Clematis × *aromatica*	*Clematis recta*	'Blue Angel' (syn.	André'
Clematis × *bonstedtii*	'Purpurea'	'Blekitny Aniol')	'Madame Julia
'Crépuscule'	*Clematis rehderiana*	'Blue Boy'	Correvon'
Clematis campaniflora	*Clematis serratifolia*	'Comtesse de	'Madame Grangé'
Clematis crispa	*Clematis songarica*	Bouchaud'	'Margaret Hunt'
Clematis × *durandii*	*Clematis tangutica*	'Duchess of Albany'	'Margot Koster'
Clematis × *eriostemon*	*Clematis texensis*	'Dorothy Walton'	'Minuet'
Clematis flammula	*Clematis tibetana*	'Elvan'	'Pagoda'
Clematis fusca var.	*Clematis* × *triternata*	'Ernest Markham'	'Paul Farges'
violacea	'Rubromarginata'	'Etoile Rose'	'Perle d'Azur'
Clematis heracleifolia	*Clematis viticella*	'Etoile Violette'	'Perrin's Pride'
var. *davidiana*	'Mary Rose'	'Gipsy Queen'	'Pink Fantasy'
'Wyevale'	'Purpurea Plena	'Gravetye Beauty'	'Polish Spirit'
Clematis hirsutissima	Elegans'	'Guiding Star'	'Prince Charles'
Clematis integrifolia	'Abundance'	'Hagley Hybrid'	'Princess Diana'
'Alba'	'Alba Luxurians'	'Huldine'	'Rhapsody'
'Rosea'	'Arabella'	'Jackmanii'	'Rouge Cardinal'
Clematis × *jouiniana*	'Ascotiensis'	'Jackmanii Superba'	'Royal Velours'
'Praecox'	'Betty Corning'	'John Huxtable'	'Venosa Violacea'
		'Kermesina'	'Victoria'
		'Lady Betty Balfour'	'Ville de Lyon'

PRUNING GROUP 3

This group comprises all the species and large-flowered clematis that bloom from mid- to late summer, in which the stems grow and bloom in the same season. Many, including herbaceous types and texensis, die back during winter. They can all be hard-pruned in late winter or early spring every year, cutting back all stems to within 30cm of the ground. Prune as growth starts so that you can cut stems back to good buds.

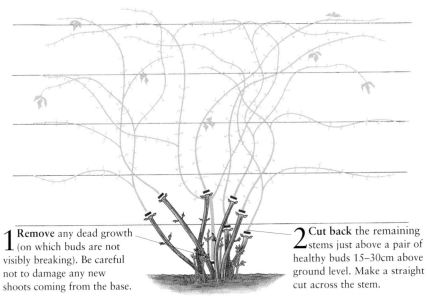

1 **Remove** any dead growth (on which buds are not visibly breaking). Be careful not to damage any new shoots coming from the base.

2 **Cut back** the remaining stems just above a pair of healthy buds 15–30cm above ground level. Make a straight cut across the stem.

HOW TO PRUNE TO PROLONG FLOWERING

It is possible to extend the flowering season of clematis in Pruning Group 3, such as the viticellas, and a few of those in Pruning Group 2, such as large-flowered 'Niobe', by additional pruning during the growing season. Once the young shoots have grown to 30–50cm long in early summer, prune half of them back to encourage more new shoots that will bear their flowers later than the first. Remember that many Group 2 large-flowered hybrids produce a few blooms later in the summer anyway, so this technique is only worth trying for those that do not have a second flush.

▶ EXTENDING FLOWERING ON A VITICELLA
Regular pruning reduces the shoots to within 30cm of the ground. In early summer, prune half back again, cutting to just above a node.

BEFORE EXTRA PRUNING   AFTER EXTRA PRUNING

GROWING YOUR OWN PLANTS

CLEMATIS CAN BE PROPAGATED from cuttings or seed, or by layering. Taking cuttings is the most popular method and produces plants identical to their parent. Named cultivars or hybrids, such as 'Nelly Moser', can only be reproduced from cuttings or by layering. Sowing seed from any of the species usually produces offspring that are the same, but from other clematis it is impossible to be sure what characteristics the new plants will have – which can lead to exciting results.

TAKING CUTTINGS

For a first attempt at taking cuttings, choose a clematis that roots readily, such as one of the montanas or *Clematis tibetana*. There are several methods, but taking "internodal" cuttings (*below*) is the most reliable. A node is the joint between a leaf or leaves and the stem, so taking an internodal cutting means severing the stem in between pairs of leaves.

WHICH CLEMATIS

EASY TO ROOT
Alpinas
Montanas
Clematis tangutica
Clematis tibetana
'Bill MacKenzie'

MODERATELY EASY
Macropetalas
Viticellas
Large-flowered hybrids

DIFFICULT TO ROOT
Clematis armandii
Texensis

CHOOSING MATERIAL
Cuttings are best taken in early summer from new stems. Cut a growing shoot and select the best cuttings from it. Several cuttings can be made from a length of new growth, using all but the soft tip and hard, woody stem at the base.

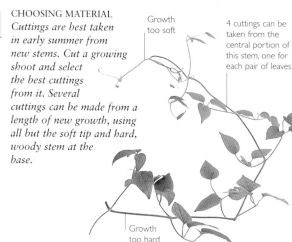

Growth too soft

4 cuttings can be taken from the central portion of this stem, one for each pair of leaves

Growth too hard

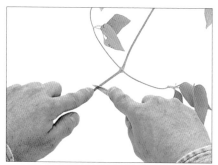

1 Make the first cut on the main stem between 2 leaf joints (nodes), about 4–5cm below the top node, using a clean, sharp knife or craft knife (preferably with a fresh blade).

2 Make the second cut directly, or a few millimetres, above the node. To make the operation safer, press the knife against a hard, clean surface as you cut.

3 Trim off the leaves on one side of the stem to lessen the effects of transpiration (water loss through leaves). This may not be necessary for clematis with very small or fine leaves.

4 Unless the leaves are very small, cut away one leaflet and its stalk. Always leave at least 2 leaflets to sustain the cutting through its rooting period.

Make sure cutting is correctly labelled

5 Dip the stem base in hormone rooting powder. Insert into a pot or tray filled with a mixture of peat substitute, sharp sand and perlite (*see Practical Tips, below*). Water in.

6 Label and date the cuttings and place in good light out of direct sun in a windowsill propagator or cover the pot with a plastic bag. Rooting should occur after about 6 weeks.

POTTING UP A ROOTED CUTTING

When the roots have developed, and start to show at the base of the pot, pot the cuttings individually into 9cm pots using general potting compost. Water well and place in a cold frame or sheltered spot. Keep out of direct sun for the first 7–10 days. Check regularly and, when the roots fill this pot, repot into a 2-litre container. Grow on for a year before planting out.

Roots should be reasonably well-developed before potting

PRACTICAL TIPS

• Use a compost consisting of 50 per cent peat substitute, 25 per cent sharp sand and 25 per cent perlite.

• Cuttings taken in early summer root fastest.

• Heat at the base of the container will encourage the cuttings to root quicker.

• Keep cuttings clean and remove rotting leaves to prevent mould forming.

• Plants grown from cuttings should flower in 2 years.

SOWING SEED

Growing clematis from seed can be exciting as there is always a chance of getting a new or improved flower. Hybrids and cultivars do not come true from seed, nor will the species if they have been cross-pollinated by other clematis in your own or a neighbour's garden. To collect seed, pinch off the fluffy seedheads when they are just turning from green to brown in the autumn. They can be cold-stored, dried or sown immediately. Plants grown from seed often take longer to flower than those grown from cuttings or layers.

TYPES TO GROW FROM SEED

Clematis alpina	Clematis napaulensis
Clematis campaniflora	Clematis orientalis
Clematis chiisanensis	Clematis pitcheri
Clematis chrysochoma	Clematis recta
Clematis crispa	Clematis rehderiana
Clematis flammula	Clematis serratifolia
Clematis fusca	Clematis songarica
Clematis integrifolia	Clematis tangutica
Clematis japonica	Clematis viorna
Clematis koreana	Clematis virginiana
Clematis macropetala	Clematis viticella
Clematis montana	

1 **To collect seed,** pick off the seedheads from the plant. Separate the fluffy strands. You can pinch off the tails but be sure to keep the swollen base which contains the seed.

2 **Holding the seeds** between your thumb and forefinger, spread them evenly across a gritty seed compost. Water in well and cover with a layer of grit or sharp sand.

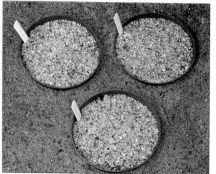

3 **Label each pot** and place in a cold frame, plunging the pots, if possible, into sand to maintain an even temperature and moisture. Seedlings may take two years to emerge.

4 **Prick out the seedlings** when large enough to handle (with at least 4 leaves). Use a widger to remove them and hold them by the lowest leaves, not the fragile stem.

The seedling needs
lots of light to
make good growth

Make sure
that the pot
is labelled

GROWING ON
*Initial shade helps the
seedling's roots to re-
establish. Then it needs
good light, preferably
in a greenhouse. When
the roots fill the pot,
transfer to a 2-litre
pot and grow on
before planting out.*

5 Using a dibber, plant each seedling into a 9cm pot filled with potting compost; firm in gently. Water in, label, and grow on under glass, providing shade for the first 10 days.

LAYERING

Bury a stem from the parent plant in the ground or in a pot filled with potting compost, making a notch to induce roots to grow. Wait 1–2 years for good roots to develop (the shoot will offer strong resistance if gently tugged), then sever the new plant from its parent and pot up or plant out.

BEST TYPES FOR LAYERING

Alpinas, macropetalas, montanas, viticellas, large-flowered hybrids, *Clematis armandii*, *Clematis campaniflora*, *Clematis cirrhosa*, *Clematis florida*, *Clematis texensis*, *Clematis tibetana*, *Clematis tangutica*, *Clematis serratifolia*

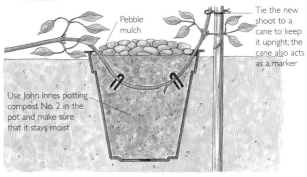

Stem is bent
away from
parent plant

Mulch of well-rotted manure
or leafmould to
conserve moisture

Wire hooks
pin down
the stem

Soil enriched
with compost

1-year-old shoot
buried, leaving
15–30cm above
ground tied
to a cane

◀ IN THE GROUND
*Using a sharp knife,
make a small notch in
the stem bark about
5cm below a leaf joint
(node). Then pin the
stem 5–10cm below
the ground with wire
hooks. Mulch to keep
the soil moist.*

▶ SUNKEN POT
*Layering in a pot,
sunk in the ground,
makes lifting the new
plant easy, but the
compost inside is
liable to dry out.
Mulch well – pebbles
are most effective –
and check the
moisture levels
regularly.*

Pebble
mulch

Tie the new
shoot to a
cane to keep
it upright; the
cane also acts
as a marker

Use John Innes potting
compost No. 2 in the
pot and make sure
that it stays moist

A GALLERY OF CLEMATIS

Arranged according to flowering time, this gallery begins with species that bloom in late winter and early spring, and progresses through the spring-flowering clematis to the large-flowered hybrids of summer, closing with the species that bloom in autumn. All are fully hardy unless marked as only frost hardy (✸✸).

EARLY-FLOWERING SPECIES

THE WINTER AND EARLY SPRING-FLOWERING SPECIES grow and bloom best in milder areas where the buds are less prone to frost damage; both *Clematis armandii* and *C. cirrhosa* benefit from the protection of a sheltered wall. No pruning is necessary since all these clematis are in Pruning Group 1 (*see p.40*).

***Clematis armandii* ✸✸**
Evergreen; almond-scented flowers in early spring; to 6m.

***Clematis cirrhosa* ✸✸**
Evergreen; may flower all winter and reaches 3–4m.

Clematis koreana
Spring flowers vary from yellow to deep red. To 3–4m.

MORE CHOICES

Clematis armandii 'Apple Blossom' Pink buds
Clematis cirrhosa var. *balearica* ♀ Ferny foliage
Clematis cirrhosa 'Freckles' ♀ Maroon-spotted flowers

KEY
✸✸ *Frost hardy, down to -5°C*
♀ *RHS Award of Garden Merit*

***Clematis* 'Pruinina'**
Seedheads follow the splayed bells; will grow to 2–3m.

***Clematis indivisa* ✸✸**
Fragrant evergreen, best grown under glass. To 3–4m.

◀ SHADES OF BLUE *The hybrid 'Mrs Cholmondeley' flowers from late spring through summer.*

ALPINAS AND MACROPETALAS

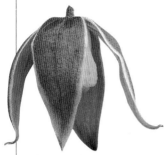

Clematis alpina 'Rosy Pagoda'
Pretty pink bells; up to 3–4m.

THE SMALL NODDING FLOWERS of these clematis start to open in early spring – those of the alpinas are single, while those of the macropetalas are semi-double. Fluffy seedheads follow the flowers. Both kinds are very hardy and can be planted against north and east walls, where they will reach 2–4m. They also look attractive trained to climb into small trees or allowed to scramble through shrubs (*see p.20*). No pruning is needed as all belong to Pruning Group 1 (*see p.40*), but they can be cut back if necessary immediately after flowering.

Clematis alpina 'Columbine'
Of the blue alpina cultivars, this is the closest to the wild species; grows to 2–3m.

Clematis alpina 'Willy'
Pale, mauve-pink flowers; sometimes has a second flush in summer; can reach 4m.

Clematis alpina 'Helsingborg' ♀
Unusual rosy purple; among the darkest alpinas. To 3m.

Clematis alpina 'Ruby'
Subtle, dusky red blooms. Vigorous, reaching 3–4m, with good repeat flowering.

Clematis alpina 'Tage Lundell'
Rich-coloured bells look good against a pale background; 3m.

Clematis alpina 'Frances Rivis' ♀
The blue petals are extra long and twisting; grows to 4m.

Clematis macropetala
'Maidwell Hall' ♀
Fluffy seedheads follow the
blue flowers. Grows to 2.5m.

Clematis macropetala
'Markham's Pink' ♀
Grows up to 3m; produces
masses of lantern flowers.

'Rosie O'Grady'
Canadian-bred hybrid with
large flowers in a delicate
shade of pink. Climbs to 3m.

Clematis macropetala
Extremely hardy and thrives
in all aspects; seedheads last
several months. Up to 3.5m.

'White Swan'
A fairly compact plant that
does not start flowering until
late spring. Will grow to 2m.

MORE CHOICES

Clematis alpina
    'Constance' Rich purple-
    pink flowers
    'Frankie' Mid-blue
    'Pink Flamingo' Pale pink
    subsp. *sibirica* **'White
    Moth'** Pure white
Clematis macropetala
    'Lagoon' (syn. 'Blue
    Lagoon') Deep blue

THE MONTANAS

Clematis montana
'Elizabeth' ♀
Vanilla scent; can reach 10m.

INTRODUCED FROM THE HIMALAYAS in 1831, *Clematis montana* has become one of the most popular of all clematis, particularly for covering walls and fences. The montanas are vigorous, reaching 6–10m or even more if conditions are favourable. The wild species has white flowers, 5–6cm across, but it has given rise to many other forms, some with pink and purple-pink petals, often with bronze-tinted young foliage. Their flowering time is from late spring to early summer. They need little or no pruning (*see Pruning Group 1, p.40*) and flower best in full sun.

Clematis montana
'Fragrant Spring'
Scented flowers; young leaves
tinged purple. Climbs to 10m.

Clematis montana
'Tetrarose' ♀
Extra-large scented flowers and
bronze-green leaves; up to 8m.

Clematis montana var.
sericea ♀
Best flower form but lacks
scent. To 8m. Syn. 'Spooneri'.

Clematis montana var.
rubens ♀
Very hardy; a little variable in
colour. Climbs to 8m.

Clematis montana
The wild species has scented,
white flowers; ideal growing
through trees. Climbs to 12m.

Clematis montana
'Warwickshire Rose'
The most vigorous of the
bronze-leaved forms. To 10m.

Clematis montana
f. *grandiflora* ♀
Blooms up to 8cm wide on a
plant that can grow to 11m.

Clematis chrysocoma
Less rampant, reaching about
2m; related to *C. montana*
but with rounder leaves.

MORE CHOICES

Clematis montana
   'Broughton Star' Creamy
      pink, semi-double
   'Freda' ♀ Pink with
      bronze foliage
   'Marjorie' Pink, semi-
      double
   'Mayleen' Scented pink
      flowers, bronze foliage
   'Picton's Variety' Deep
      pink flowers with
      bronze foliage
   var. *wilsonii* White

EARLY LARGE-FLOWERED HYBRIDS

Clematis patens
Used in breeding many in this group. Grows to about 2m.

THE INTRODUCTION FROM JAPAN in 1836 of *Clematis patens*, and later of *C. lanuginosa* and *C. florida* from China, gave rise to an enormous number of large-flowered hybrids between 1860 and 1890. This group has been divided over the following pages according to colour and includes mid-season types, with a separate section for double-flowered hybrids. Most of these clematis flower in late spring and early summer, with many producing a repeat flush of flowers in late summer. All require light pruning (*see Pruning Group 2, pp.41–42*).

'Lady Londesborough'
Bred in 1869 and resembles *C. patens*; flowering season is rather short. Grows to 2m.

'Mrs Cholmondeley' ♀
A clematis that will flower all summer with light pruning. It will climb up to 3–4m.

'William Kennett'
Free-flowering, with blooms 18cm across. Easy to grow and vigorous, reaching 3m.

'Richard Pennell' ♀
Prominent stamens and undulating petals with rosy pink shading. Climbs to 3m.

'Lady Northcliffe'
A popular clematis for its long flowering season and deep blue blooms. Up to 2m.

'Elsa Späth' ♀
Easy to grow and flowers well from mid- to late season. Generally reaches 2.5–3m.

'Blue Ravine'
This is a reliable new clematis that has petals marked with strong veining. Grows to 3m.

'The President' ♀
In flower nearly all summer, this is an old favourite from 1876. It will grow to 3–4m.

'Lasurstern' ♀
The plant becomes smothered in flowers, with a few blooms later in the year. Up to 3m.

'Mrs Hope'
Large flowers up to 15cm in diameter with striking deep red anthers. Climbs to 3.5m.

'Ramona'
Large blooms with a deep red centre. Flowers best in full sun and grows to 3–4m.

'H. F. Young' ♀
Nearly perfect blue flowers with a contrasting eye of cream stamens. Up to 2.5m.

'W. E. Gladstone'
Flowers lightly over a long time, with huge blooms up to 25cm across. Can reach 3.5m.

MORE CHOICES

'Beauty of Richmond' Pale mauve
'Général Sikorski' ♀ Very lovely blue
'Haku-ôkan' Violet
'Joan Picton' A mass of pinky-mauve flowers
'Kathleen Wheeler' Blue with purple midribs
'Lady Caroline Nevill' Soft blue
'Mrs P. B. Truax' Pale blue
'North Star' (syn. 'Pôhjanael') Deep blue

'John Warren'
Large flowers up to 18cm in diameter with dark pink edges to pointed petals. Up to 3m.

'Lincoln Star'
A strong, reliable variety that flowers prolifically over its entire height of about 3m.

'Charissima'
This clematis has lovely large, pale flowers with complex cerise veining. Grows to 2.5m.

'Mrs N. Thompson'
A compact clematis, reaching about 2m, with blue-purple flowers with a deep pink bar.

'Dr Ruppel' ♀
A striking deep rose colour that is not for the faint-hearted. Reaches about 3m.

'The Vagabond'
The rich purple and crimson of the velvety petals offsets the cream stamens. To 2.5m.

'Carnaby'
An ideal container clematis, growing to 2.5m, with flowers of a glowing deep pink.

'Fireworks' ♀
More vigorous than 'Mrs N. Thompson' with flowers that live up to its name. About 3m.

'Nelly Moser' ♀
The flowers of this popular clematis keep their colour best in shade. Climbs to about 3m.

MORE STRIPED-FLOWERED CHOICES

'Andromeda' Semi-double pale pink with darker stripe

'Asao' Deep pink with paler midribs

'Barbara Jackman' Deep purple-blue with contrasting magenta bar

'Carnival Queen' Pink with deep cerise edges

'Etoile de Malicorne' Mauve with red-purple bar

'Fair Rosamond' Pale blush pink with deeper bar that fades; some fragrance

'John Paul II' (syn. 'Jan Pawel II') Pale pink with darker stripe

'Keith Richardson' Purple-red with paler midribs

'Masquerade' (syn. 'Maskarad') Pale pink with deeper-coloured bar

'Mrs James Mason' Violet-blue with deep red bar

'Pink Fantasy' Small pink with darker bar

'Sealand Gem' Lavender-blue with dark pink bar

'Bees' Jubilee' ♀
A compact clematis, growing to only 1.8m and therefore ideal for containers.

'Miss Bateman' ♀
Produces a single but profuse
flowering. A compact
clematis, reaching about 2m.

'Snow Queen'
Flowers well even when young
and has lovely, wavy-edged
blooms. Grows to 2.5m.

'Barbara Dibley'
Flowers well in sun but
retains colour intensity best in
light shade. Can reach 3m.

'Guernsey Cream'
Blooms prolifically and is one
of the earliest hybrids of all
to flower. Will climb to 2.5m.

'Vino'
Produces the finest show of
its vibrant flowers if grown in
full sun. Climbs to 3m.

'Gillian Blades' ♀
A compact grower and one of
the best of the early white-
flowered hybrids. Up to 2.5m.

'Marie Boisselot' ♀
Flowers tend to be produced high up on this clematis, which can reach 3.5m.

'Jackmanii Rubra'
Free-flowering; first blooms may be semi-double (*see* Mrs George Jackman, *p.61*). To 3m.

'Moonlight'
Provides light cover; the delicate flower colouring is best in shade. Grows to 2.5m.

'Henryi' ♀
A classic clematis, bred as early as 1858 and deservedly still popular. Will reach 3.5m.

'Niobe' ♀
A few stems can be hard-pruned to extend its flowering season. Grows to 3m.

MORE CHOICES

'Corona' Pinkish-red
'Crimson King' Dark red
'Cardinal Wyszinski' (syn. 'Kardynal Wyszyński') Purple-red
'Maureen' Violet-purple with red midribs
'Monte Cassino' Velvety red-purple
'Edith' ♀ A short-growing white
'James Mason' White with dark stamens
'Silver Moon' Silver-grey

EARLY DOUBLE HYBRIDS

THE SHOWY FLOWERS PRODUCED by this type of clematis appeared originally on sports of large-flowered hybrids. (Sports are natural mutations that exhibit differences from the norm.) Double flowers occur only in the early-flowered hybrids and usually just on the first flowers that appear in early summer; any subsequent flowers are single. Some hybrids have just two rows of petals and these are known as "semi-double". Early double hybrids require light pruning (*see Pruning Group 2, pp.41–42*); pruning too hard results in later, single flowers.

'Kathleen Dunford'
Semi-double, so the stamens
still stand out. Reaches 2.5m.

'Belle of Woking'
A good grower, up to 2.5m,
with a few flowers later in the
year that may also be double.

'Multi Blue'
The unusually formed flowers
of this clematis are long-
lasting. Grows to 2.5m.

'Vyvyan Pennell' ♀
One of the best-known
doubles, with velvety-textured
flowers. Reaches 2.5–3m.

'Duchess of Edinburgh'
After very cold weather, the
flowers can be quite green
when they first open. To 2.5m.

'Mrs George Jackman' ♀
A semi-double which has a
longer season when planted
in light shade. Up to 2.5m.

'Countess of Lovelace'
This has more regularly
spaced petals than most
doubles. Grows to 2.5m.

'Proteus'
The flowers look best against
a variegated or golden-leaved
shrub. Grows to 2.5m.

'Royalty' ♀
A deep violet that contrasts
well with soft yellow flowers
or foliage. Reaches about 2m.

MORE CHOICES

'Arctic Queen' Pure white
'Beauty of Worcester' Mid-blue
'Chalcedony' Pale blue
'Kiri Te Kanawa' Deep blue
'Miss Crawshay' Pinky-mauve, semi-double
'Mrs Spencer Castle' Mauve-pink, semi-double
'Sylvia Denny' White, semi-double
'Violet Elizabeth' Mauve-pink

LATE LARGE-FLOWERED HYBRIDS

'Hagley Hybrid'
The subtle colour is suited to planting in shade. Up to 2.5m.

T HE EXUBERANT FLOWERS of these clematis enliven any garden in late summer and early autumn. If grown against walls, large-flowered hybrids are best given the support of a climbing rose or other shrub, so that training the shoots is not so necessary. In the border, they look superb when allowed to twine in and out of fuchsias, buddlejas and other late summer shrubs. Like all clematis that flower after mid-summer, these belong to Pruning Group 3 (*see pp.42–43*), and should be cut back to within 30cm of the ground in late winter or early spring.

'Huldine'
The upward-facing flowers are at their best towards the end of summer. Climbs 5–6m.

'Ernest Markham' ♀
A tall clematis, up to 4m, with vivid magenta blooms. It does well in full sun.

'Ville de Lyon'
Flowers freely, especially if lightly pruned rather than cut right back. Grows to 3m.

'Comtesse de Bouchaud' ♀
Old, reliable variety that has masses of vibrant, mauve-pink blooms. Grows to 3m.

'Ascotiensis' ♀
A strong-growing cultivar, reaching about 3m, with a very long flowering season.

'Jackmanii' ♀
The most popular variety for cottage gardens, with velvety, purple flowers. Grows to 3m.

'Rouge Cardinal'
The deep crimson blooms
have an especially rich,
velvety texture. Grows to 3m.

'Victoria'
A vigorous clematis that
grows well in cold climates,
reaching about 3–4m.

'Prince Charles'
A reliable, long-flowering
and compact hybrid, seldom
reaching more than 2m.

'Gipsy Queen' ♀
The tapering bases of the
petals make the flowers stand
out well. Grows to 3m.

'Madame Grangé' ♀
Vigorous and free-flowering;
petals are grey and woolly on
the reverse. Grows to 3m.

MORE CHOICES

'Blue Angel' (syn. 'Blekitny
Aniol') Pale blue
'Dorothy Walton' Lilac
'Guiding Star' Violet-purple
with plum bar
'John Huxtable' White
'Lady Betty Balfour'
Purple-blue
'Margaret Hunt' Lilac
'Madame Edouard André' ♀
Deep red
'Perle d'Azur' Sky blue
'Perrin's Pride' Purple
'Rhapsody' Electric blue

HERBACEOUS CLEMATIS

Clematis × aromatica
A hybrid with fragrant flowers on a mound 1–2m high.

These CLEMATIS DO NOT TWINE. They vary from types such as *Clematis heracleifolia* that can be grown as self-supporting ground cover, to those such as *C. integrifolia* and *C. recta* that tend to lean on other plants. All are attractive in mixed plantings – support floppy types with canes or plant rings, or allow them to hang over retaining walls or sprawl at the front of borders. Herbaceous clematis usually have much smaller flowers than other types, sometimes fragrant. As for most herbaceous plants, prune hard in late winter (*see Pruning Group 3, pp.42–43*).

Clematis integrifolia
Flower petals have a pronounced twist. Plants barely reach 1m in height.

Clematis × bonstedtii
'Crépuscule'
Tiny, tube-like flowers have a sweet fragrance; grows to 1m.

Clematis × jouiniana
'Praecox' ♀
Makes vigorous ground cover, scrambling for 4–5m.

Clematis recta 'Purpurea'
Purplish-grey young foliage
and masses of small white
flowers. Grows to 1.5m.

Clematis recta
This species reaches 1.5m but
tends to flop; it mixes well in
herbaceous plantings.

Clematis integrifolia
'Rosea' ✿
Has larger flowers than the
species (*opposite*). Up to 1m.

Clematis x *durandii* ✿
Long-flowering and superb
for growing through a small
shrub. Grows to about 1.5m.

Clematis heracleifolia var.
davidiana 'Wyevale' ✿
Bold, vine-like foliage and
fragrant flowers. Up to 1m.

MORE CHOICES

Clematis heracleifolia **var.**
davidiana Very fragrant
Clematis hirsutissima
Needs dry alpine
conditions
Clematis integrifolia 'Alba'
White form of the species
(*opposite*)
Clematis songarica Sturdy,
almost shrub-like species
with white flowers
'Arabella' Small blue
flowers all summer

VITICELLAS AND TEXENSIS

'Minuet' ♀
Starry flowers with mauve markings on white. Up to 3m.

THE "VIRGIN'S BOWER" – *Clematis viticella* – is a native of southern Europe and has been known in gardens since 1569. It has small, purple, bell-like flowers in late summer and has been much used in hybridizing. *Clematis texensis*, a small species from the United States with scarlet, urn-shaped flowers, is responsible for the red tones in all red hybrids. Viticella and texensis cultivars and hybrids are easy to grow and particularly suitable for combining with shrubs. All reach 4–5m and need hard pruning (*see Pruning Group 3, pp.42–43*).

Clematis viticella 'Purpurea Plena Elegans' ♀
The double flowers last for several weeks. Grows to 3m.

'Madame Julia Correvon' ♀
Prolific and long-flowering, with larger blooms than most viticellas. Grows to 3.5m.

'Venosa Violacea' ♀
Uniquely patterned flowers show up well against plants with silver foliage. Up to 3m.

'Etoile Violette' ♀
Masses of dark flowers that look best offset by a pale-leaved plant. Can reach 4m.

'Abundance'
Profuse flowering and the best pinkish-red clematis in this group. Grows to 3m.

'Pagoda'
A superb clematis with deeply reflexed petals with a greyish-pink reverse. Grows to 2m.

'Kermesina'
The intense crimson blooms look stunning in sunlight. Generally reaches about 3m.

'Alba Luxurians' ♀
White flowers with a dark eye; the first flush has green markings. Grows to 3m.

'Betty Corning'
American-bred with reflexed flowers that have a slight fragrance. Grows to 2.5m.

'Duchess of Albany' ♀
The pretty, pink, tulip-shaped flowers stand up well above small shrubs. Grows to 3m.

'Gravetye Beauty'
The deepest red flowers but the weakest-growing of the texensis; it can grow to 3m.

Clematis texensis
The species, up to 3m, is rare in cultivation, but has been much used in hybridizing.

'Lady Bird Johnson'
Lovely pitcher-shaped flowers with petals with a contrasting, pale reverse. Grows to 2–3m.

'Etoile Rose'
Needs a tall support to display the bells well; flowers for 3 months. Grows to 2.5m.

MORE CHOICES

Clematis viticella
  'Mary Rose' Double smoky purple
'Black Prince' Purple
'Elvan' Small blue-purple
'Margot Koster' Deep rosy pink
'Polish Spirit' ♀ Rich purple-blue
'Princess Diana' Deep cherry pink
'Royal Velours' ♀ Rich purple-red

MID- TO LATE-FLOWERING SPECIES

Clematis florida 'Sieboldii'
Looks rather like a passion
flower; can grow to 3m. ❋❋

SOME OF THE MOST INTERESTING CLEMATIS are
included in this group. Apart from *Clematis
florida*, a parent of many of the large-flowered
hybrids, they are mostly small-flowered, hardy and
bloom from mid-summer onwards. All except
C. florida require hard pruning (*see Pruning Group
3, pp.42–43*). *Clematis tibetana* (*see p.26*) and
C. tangutica are familiar for their thick-petalled
yellow bells and fluffy seedheads, while others, such
as *C. flammula* and *C. rehderiana*, carry bunches
of small, fragrant stars or bells.

'Paul Farges'
A vigorous hybrid that flowers
reliably for 2–3 months and
can reach 6–8m.

Clematis rehderiana ♡
Late summer flowers with a
sweet fragrance. This clematis
can reach up to 6m.

Clematis serratifolia
Pale bells are followed by
fluffy seedheads on a plant
that grows up to about 5m.

**Clematis x triternata
'Rubromarginata'** ♡
A reliable hybrid, up to 5m,
with clouds of scented flowers.

Clematis flammula
A Mediterranean species with
clouds of small, fragrant
flowers; grows up to 5m.

Clematis campaniflora
A species from Portugal with
very small, dainty bells; it can
climb to 5m.

Clematis tangutica
Carries flowers and fluffy
seedheads at the same time;
grows up to about 5m.

'Bill MacKenzie' ♀
Possibly the best yellow
autumn clematis for flowers
and seedheads; up to 7m.

Clematis x *eriostemon*
A semi-herbaceous hybrid
that flowers for 3 months.
It grows to 2.5m.

Clematis ladakhiana
A curiously coloured species
from the Himalayas, reaching
to 5m; needs full sun.

C. ladakhiana (seedhead)
The seedheads of this species
and the *Clematis tibetana*
types close the clematis year.

MORE CHOICES

Clematis addisonii Small,
rosy-purple bells
Clematis aethusifolia
Parsley-like leaves and
creamy bells
Clematis crispa Pale blue
bells
Clematis florida 'Flore Pleno'
Double green and white ✱✱
Clematis fusca var. *violacea*
Hairy purple-brown bells
Clematis tibetana (syn.
C. orientalis 'Sherriffii')
Yellow bells and greyish
foliage

INDEX

ACKNOWLEDGMENTS

Picture research Christine Rista

Special photography Richard Surman, Peter Anderson

Illustrations Karen Cochrane

Index Hilary Bird

Dorling Kindersley would like to thank:
All staff at the RHS, in particular Susanne Mitchell, Karen Wilson and Barbara Haynes at Vincent Square, also the team at the propagation unit, Wisley; staff at Burford House Gardens, Tenbury Wells, Worcestershire; Agriframes Ltd (for supplying drainpipe trellis, p.29).

The Royal Horticultural Society
To learn more about the work of the Society, visit the RHS on the Internet at **www.rhs.org.uk**. Information includes news of events around the country, a horticultural database, international plant registers, results of plant trials and membership details.

Photography
The publisher would also like to thank the following for their kind permission to reproduce their photographs:
(key: t=top, c=centre, b=below, l=left, r=right)

Mark Bolton: 54bl
Neil Campbell-Sharp: 20cr, 67tr
Charles Chesshire: 55cl
Eric Crichton Photos: jacket front tl, 4br, 7b, 8b, 8t, 9, 15tr, 15tl, 19br, 52bc, 56bl, 59tr, 65bl
DK Special Photography: Dave King 38bc
The Garden Picture Library: Howard Rice 2, 48; Jerry Pavia 26; John Glover 65tr, 67cc
John Glover: 24bl
Harpur Garden Library: 7c, 10r, 49cc
Andrew Lawson: 14, 17tr, 19tl, 20bl, 21br
Clive Nichols Garden Pictures: Pam Schwert/S. Kreutzberger 24r
Photos Horticultural: 37br, 37bl 60bl, 61tr, 63bl, 63tl, 65tl, 69tr
Photo Lamontagne: 18
Harry Smith Collection: 25r, 25l, 37tr, 49br, 54cc, 63bc, 64tl, 64cr, 67cr, 67bl, 68bl, 69bc, 69bl
Richard Surman: 38br